Why do insects have six legs?

And other questions about evolution and classification

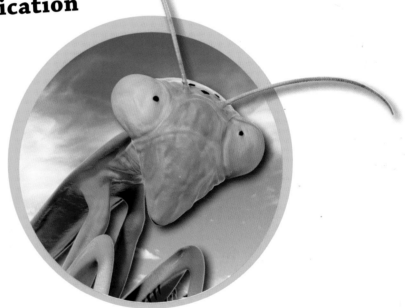

W
FRANKLIN WATTS
LONDON·SYDNEY

Franklin Watts

This edition copyright © Franklin Watts 2016

IBSN 978 1 4451 5085 7

Dewey number: 595.7

Series Editor: Julia Bird

Packaged by: Dynamo Limited

Picture credits

Key: **t**=top, **m**=middle, **b**=bottom, **l**=left, **r**=right

Cover: Dja65/Shutterstock, 3D art: Dynamo Limited

p1 3D art: Dynamo Limited; p3 Dja65/Shutterstock; p4 **t** BlueRingMedia/Shutterstock, p4 **b** Dr. Morley Read/Shutterstock; p5 **t** Tin Tran/Shutterstock, p5 **b** ChinellatoPhoto/Shutterstock; p6 fly Mircea Bezergheanu/Shutterstock; p7 dragonfly Joanna Zopoth-Lipiejko/Shutterstock, p7 mayfly Solodov Alexey/Shutterstock, p7 leaf insect Sam DCruz/Shutterstock, p7 termites smuay/Shutterstock, p7 earwig Tomatito/Shutterstock, p7 bristletail Claudio Divizia/Shutterstock, p7 flea Cosmin Manci/Shutterstock, p7 lice Henrik Larsson/Shutterstock, p7 thrip Katarina Christenson/Shutterstock; p8 **t** Marques/Shutterstock, p8 **b** Kidsana Maimeetook/Shutterstock; p9 **t** Dynamo Limited, p9 **b** Katarina Christenson/Shutterstock; p10 **t** Cosmin Manci/Shutterstock, p10 **b** Biehler Michael/Shutterstock; p11 **t** WhyMePhoto/Shutterstock, p11 **b** John Michael Evan Potter/Shutterstock; p12 **t** Kingfisher/Shutterstock, p12 **bl** Michael Warwick/Shutterstock; p12 **br** Sari ONeal/Shutterstock; p13 **t** Ken Lucas/Ardea, p13 **b** Dr. Morley Read/Shutterstock; p14 **t** Wong Hock Weng/Shutterstock, p14 **b** Lehrer/Shutterstock; p15 **t** vblinov/Shutterstock, p15 **b** Dirk Ercken/Shutterstock; p16 **t** BlueRingMedia/Shutterstock, p16 **b** StevenRussellSmithPhotos/Shutterstock; p17 **t** StevenRussellSmithPhotos/Shutterstock, p17 **b** Perry Correll/Shutterstock; p18 **t** Radu Bercan/Shutterstock, p18 **b** Mircea Bezergheanu/Shutterstock; p19 **t** Dr. Morley Read/Shutterstock, p19 **b** Milkovasa/Shutterstock; p20 **t** Suede Chen/Shutterstock, p20 **b** Dynamo Limited; p21 **t** Sue Robinson/Shutterstock, p21 **b** chinahbzyg/Shutterstock; p22 **t** Yaping/Shutterstock, p22 **b** Rosa Frei/Shutterstock; p23 **t** Rasmus Holmboe Dahl/Shutterstock, p23 **b** Kletr/Shutterstock; p24 **t** Renato Arap/Shutterstock, p24 **b** Symbiot/Shutterstock; p25 **t** EcoPrint/Shutterstock, p25 **b** Pablo Hidalgo/Shutterstock; p26 **t** Roger Meerts/Shutterstock, p26 **b** Ian Grainger/Shutterstock; p27 **tl** D. Kucharski K. Kucharska/Shutterstock, p27 **tr** Evgeniy Ayupov/Shutterstock, p27 **b** Florian Andronache/Shutterstock; p28 **t** Christian Musat/Shutterstock, p28 **b** Nicky Rhodes/Shutterstock; p29 **t** Henrik Larsson/Shutterstock, p29 **m** Steve McWilliam/Shutterstock, p29 **b** p.studio66/Shutterstock; p30 **t** Protasov AN/Shutterstock, p30 **m** xpixel/Shutterstock, p30 **b** Graham Prentice/Shutterstock

Printed in China

Franklin Watts
An imprint of
Hachette Children's Group
Part of The Watts Publishing Group
Carmelite House
50 Victoria Embankment
London EC4Y 0DZ

An Hachette UK Company
www.hachette.co.uk

www.franklinwatts.co.uk

MIX
Paper from
responsible sources
FSC® C104740
FSC
www.fsc.org

Every effort has been made by the Publishers to ensure that the websites in this book are suitable for children, and that they contain no inappropriate or offensive material. However, because of the nature of the Internet, it is impossible to guarantee that the contents of these sites will not be altered. We strongly advise that Internet access is supervised by a responsible adult.

Contents

Words in **bold** can be found in the glossary on page 31.

What is an insect?

We are surrounded by insects! Some scientists claim there are more than 200 million for every human on Earth. Insects all share certain features. They are **cold-blooded invertebrates**, have three pairs of legs and their bodies are made up of three parts. Many can fly and most lay eggs.

thorax – the wings and legs are attached to this part of the body.

abdomen

head

An insect's body is made up of the head, the thorax and the abdomen.

All insects have six legs. Any bug with more than six legs is not an insect.

How insects evolved

The oldest insect **fossils** date back 400 million years, but insects appeared on Earth even earlier than this. Insects are thought to have **evolved** from worm-like creatures. Many scientists think that a velvet worm called Peripatus could have been the link between the two because it has a mixture of both worm and insect features.

The bodies of velvet worms are divided into segments, like worms' bodies, but they have antennae and walking legs, like insects.

The first flying insects

Insects were the first animals to fly. The earliest winged insects flew through the swampy forests that covered most of our planet around 300 million years ago. They included the relatives of modern cockroaches and dragonflies. Flight helped insects to escape from **predators** and to **colonise** all parts of the Earth.

Jumping insects may have evolved wings as a way of gliding through the air. Dragonflies were among the earliest flying insects.

Modern insects

We would recognise many of the insects that crawled at the feet of the dinosaurs, or buzzed around their heads. Many modern **species**, such as caddisflies and termites, first appeared during the **Triassic** and **Jurassic periods**. Later, during the **Cretaceous period** when flowering plants evolved, insects quickly **adapted** to take advantage of these new sources of food.

Because insects are small and delicate, their fossils are rare, but many, such as this midge, have been captured in amber, the hardened resin of ancient trees.

Classification of insects

Insects are the most common creatures on Earth. There are more than one million species, and scientists think there are many more species that we have yet to discover. These are some of the main insect groups.

Beetles

Beetles are the largest group of insects. They range from stag beetles and ladybirds to fireflies. They all have hardened front wings that form a protective case over their back wings. Most have chewing mouthparts.

Bugs

There are more than 82,000 species of true bugs. Their mouthparts have evolved to become a long, needle-like beak, which they stick into plants so they can suck the plant's juices.

Cockroaches and mantids

Surprisingly, cockroaches belong in the same group as praying mantises. This is because they have similar, leathery front wings with visible veins.

Bees, wasps and ants

These **social insects** often form colonies where different members have particular jobs. Most have wings during part of their lives, but some are wingless. Many have painful bites or stings.

True flies

These insects have just one pair of wings. In place of back wings, they have drumstick-like body parts called halteres. These flap up and down during flight and help to balance and guide the fly.

Grasshoppers and crickets

Insects in this group have long back legs, built for jumping, and many have two pairs of long wings, although some are wingless. The **nymphs** look like small versions of the adults.

Butterflies and moths

Butterflies are usually active in the daytime, while most moths are **nocturnal** and have hairier bodies. Both go through complete metamorphosis (see page 16) from caterpillar to adult.

Dragon- and damselflies

The **larvae** of this group live in water, so adults are often seen around wet areas where they **mate** and lay eggs. They are strong fliers and have large eyes for spotting prey.

Mayflies

Mayflies spend most of their lives underwater, as larvae. When the adults emerge, they survive for just a day or two, to mate and lay eggs. The adults do not eat, so they have no mouthparts.

Stick and leaf insects

These insects have stick-like bodies with long legs and antennae. They move slowly and are well **camouflaged**, so predators rarely spot them. Most are wingless.

Termites

Termites look similar to ants and live in colonies, but they are related to cockroaches. Most termites eat wood, and a colony can completely destroy trees and wooden buildings.

Earwigs

Earwigs are easily recognised by their pincers. They have wings but they rarely fly. Females are good mothers – they protect their eggs and young until they can look after themselves.

pincers

Bristletails

There are about 600 species of these wingless insects, which first appeared about 400 million years ago. They have three tails that look like bristles and include silverfish and firebrats (shown left).

Fleas

Fleas are bloodsuckers and can consume up to 15 times their body weight each day. These wingless insects spend most of their lives as eggs, larvae or **pupae**. As well as causing itching, fleabites spread disease.

Lice

Lice are tiny, wingless **parasites** that feed on blood and skin. Most only live on a particular type of animal. Head lice are a common problem for humans.

Thrips

Thrips are tiny, cigar-shaped insects that feed on plants and animals, including other insects. They have wings, but are not good fliers. They are often called thunderbugs.

Insects inside and out

Insects are invertebrates. Instead of bones, they have a hard **exoskeleton** made of a strong, lightweight substance called chitin, which protects them like a suit of armour. The exoskeleton cannot grow, so young insects must shed this tough outer shell several times before they reach adult size.

An adult rhinoceros beetle has a thick exoskeleton that protects it from most predators.

spiracle

This caterpillar (a butterfly larva) has spiracles on each segment of its body.

Breathing

Insects do not have lungs, but they need to breathe to survive. They take in oxygen and get rid of carbon dioxide through openings called spiracles, which are found along the sides of their body. The spiracles are connected to a network of tubes that deliver oxygen to all parts of the insect's body.

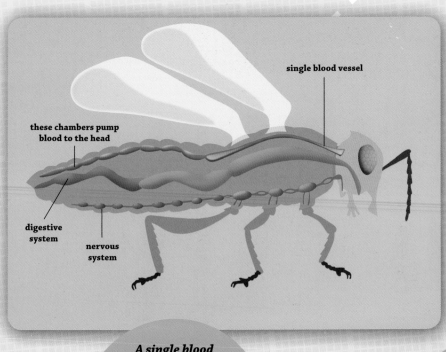

single blood vessel

these chambers pump blood to the head

digestive system

nervous system

Circulation

Insects do not have a network of arteries and veins like we do. Instead their blood flows freely around the spaces in their body. Insect blood is a yellowish-green colour and it does not carry oxygen, like ours.

A single blood vessel runs along an insect's back. The part within the abdomen is divided into sections that work like hearts and pump blood towards the head.

Mini-brains

Insects have brains in their heads, but they also have mini-brains in other parts of their bodies. This is why an insect keeps moving, even if a predator has bitten off its head. A female praying mantis sometimes bites off a male's head during mating, but he carries on mating with her because mini-brains keep his body moving.

This male praying mantis (the smaller of the two) is in danger of losing his head if his mate gets hungry!

Insect senses

Insect sense organs have evolved to suit their surroundings. Some insects have incredible hearing, while others have powerful sight or a strong sense of smell. They use these senses to find food, locate a mate or avoid predators.

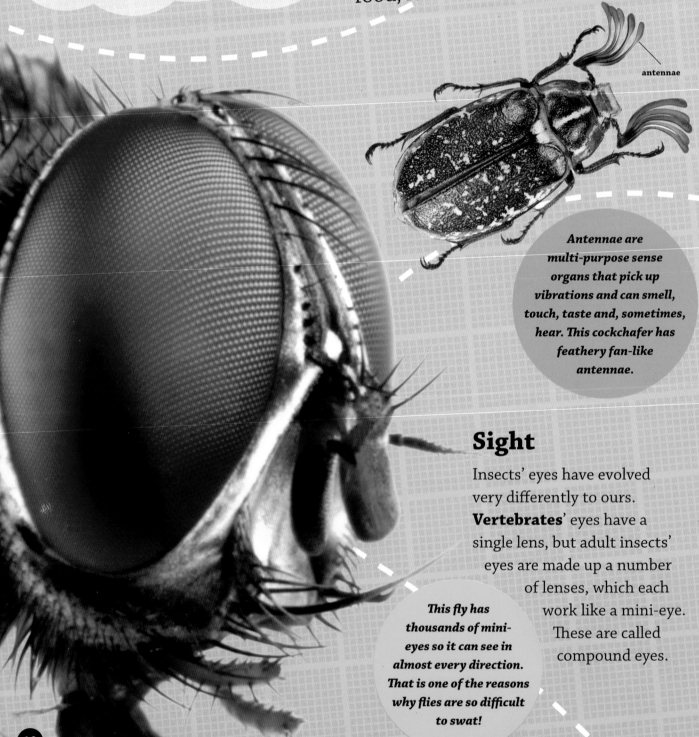

antennae

Antennae are multi-purpose sense organs that pick up vibrations and can smell, touch, taste and, sometimes, hear. This cockchafer has feathery fan-like antennae.

Sight

Insects' eyes have evolved very differently to ours. **Vertebrates'** eyes have a single lens, but adult insects' eyes are made up a number of lenses, which each work like a mini-eye. These are called compound eyes.

This fly has thousands of mini-eyes so it can see in almost every direction. That is one of the reasons why flies are so difficult to swat!

Hearing

Most insects can hear and many communicate using sound, but their ears are not where you might expect. Grasshoppers and moths have ears on their abdomens, crickets' ears are just below their knees and lacewings have ears on their wings. Some larvae have small hairs that pick up the vibrations of sound, and many insects can hear through organs on their antennae.

Moths have ears on their thorax and abdomen that can pick up the sound of bats and other predators.

Smell

Most insects have an excellent sense of smell. Female moths and butterflies produce chemicals that attract males over great distances. Social insects use their sense of smell to tell the difference between a member of the colony and an invader. Some insects, such as dung beetles, rely on smell to find their food.

Dung beetles can smell and find fresh dung within a minute of it being dropped.

Insect behaviour

Most insects have short lives, so they do not have time to learn. They are born with all the knowledge they need to survive. This 'instinctive behaviour' has developed during millions of years of evolution.

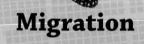

Instinct tells this female giraffe weevil to roll a leaf into a tube, where she will lay her single egg.

Migration

Monarch butterflies live in North America but they cannot survive cold winters, so they **migrate** to warmer regions in the autumn. Instinct tells them where to go. Those that live east of the Rocky Mountains head for Mexico to **hibernate** in oyamel fir trees. Those that live to the west hibernate in eucalyptus trees in California.

Monarch butterflies spend the winter on the same trees each year, even though they are from a new generation that has never been there before.

Swarming

Swarming insects include bees, ants, midges and locusts. Locusts normally live alone, but occasionally, when rain moistens the desert sand causing eggs to hatch and plants to grow, there is an explosion in numbers and the insects become overcrowded. As their back legs are touched by other locusts, it triggers a change in their behaviour and they take to the air in a huge, hungry swarm.

A locust swarm is greatly feared. A locust can eat its own weight every day, so crops can be destroyed in hours.

Mating rituals

Male insects often work hard to attract a female. Crickets produce a courtship song that can be heard over long distances by rubbing their wings together. Some male flies perform aerial dances, while others present a female with a gift of food, sometimes wrapped in silk. If the female likes the gift she will mate with him.

These mating grasshoppers have got together by recognising each other's courtship song. Each species of grasshopper has a different song and females sing more softly than males.

Insect lifecycles

Most insects lay eggs that hatch into larvae or nymphs. Insect mothers usually lay their eggs on, or close to, a good source of food and then leave them, but some stay around to guard the eggs and the young.

Teamwork

Insects that live in colonies, such as bees, wasps, ants and termites, work as a team to rear their young. The queen is the only member of the colony that lays eggs and she can produce thousands a day. Workers feed the larvae when they hatch.

This stinkbug is protecting her eggs and newly hatched young from predators.

The big queen bee (centre left) is laying an egg in each of these chambers. She is surrounded by worker bees.

Changing shape

As young insects grow, they become too big for their exoskeletons so they shed this outer shell. This is called moulting. Each time it happens the insect changes shape. An insect may moult several times before it reaches adult size. This process is called incomplete metamorphosis.

exoskeleton

This cricket is climbing out of its old exoskeleton.

wing buds

This damselfly nymph's wing buds are starting to form, so it will soon be leaving the water and searching for a mate.

Different lives

The life of a nymph can be very different to that of an adult. Dragonfly and damselfly nymphs spend their lives underwater and breathe through three leaf-shaped **gills** at the end of their tails. They may moult up to 12 times before they are ready to climb out of the water, shed their skin and take to the air on their new wings.

Metamorphosis

The eggs of some insects, including butterflies and ladybirds, hatch into larvae that look completely different to their parents. Instead of changing gradually as they become adults, these insects undergo a complete transformation, called metamorphosis, inside a case called a pupa.

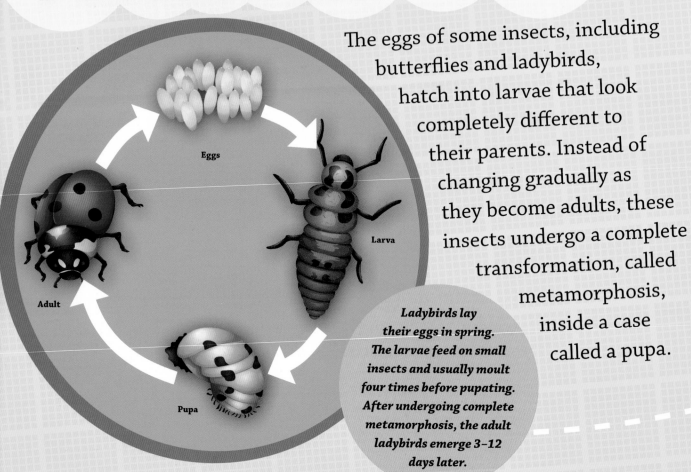

Eggs

Larva

Pupa

Adult

Ladybirds lay their eggs in spring. The larvae feed on small insects and usually moult four times before pupating. After undergoing complete metamorphosis, the adult ladybirds emerge 3–12 days later.

Forming a chrysalis

A caterpillar is an eating machine. It starts feeding as soon as it hatches. After growing for several weeks, it attaches itself to a branch and sheds its skin to reveal a soft **chrysalis**. This hardens to form a pupa.

This monarch butterfly caterpillar is turning into a chrysalis.

1 2 3 4 5 6

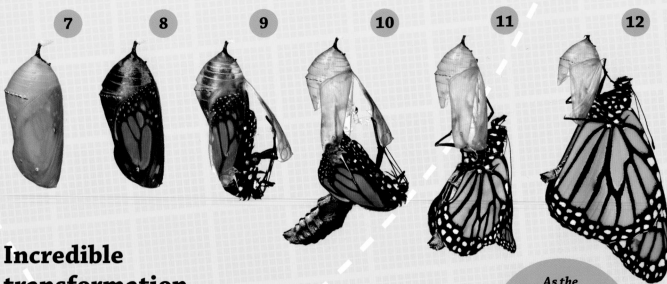

Incredible transformation

Inside the pupa the butterfly larva completely changes shape and, ten days after the chrysalis formed, the adult butterfly emerges. Some insects stay in their pupae for days, while others are there for months, or even years.

As the caterpillar's body breaks down and takes the form of a butterfly, its wings can be seen through the shell of the pupa.

These monarch caterpillars are feeding on the poisonous milkweed plant. The adult butterfly's colours warn predators that they should not try to eat it.

The next generation

When butterflies emerge from their pupae, they mate and lay eggs so the cycle can begin again. Monarch butterflies only lay eggs on the milkweed plant, which is poisonous to many animals. The caterpillars store these poisons in their bodies, which makes them, the pupae and the butterflies unappealing to predators.

Insect diets

Insects eat a huge range of foods and their mouthparts have evolved into different shapes, including needle-like beaks, sucking tubes, absorbent sponges and scissor-like jaws.

This shield bug is using its long beak to pierce the stem of a plant and suck its juices.

Feeding from flowers

Insects have been important **pollinators** of flowering plants since they first evolved during the Cretaceous period. Flowers produce a sweet liquid called nectar that attracts insects. As they drink the nectar, pollen from the male part of the flower sticks to their bodies. When the insect visits another flower the pollen is transferred to that flower's female parts and **fertilisation** occurs.

This hummingbird hawkmoth is drinking nectar from a flower through a long sucking tube called a proboscis.

Parasitic insects

Some insects, such as lice and fleas, are parasites that suck the blood of other creatures. Mosquitoes normally feed on nectar, but the females of many species bite humans and other animals because they need a meal of blood to produce eggs. Some parasitic insects, such as the ichneumon wasp, lay their eggs inside another insect. When the eggs hatch, the larvae eat their **host** from the inside out.

Ichneumon wasp larvae have eaten this caterpillar's insides. The white pupae are hanging from its skin.

Formidable killers

Some insects rank alongside nature's most fearsome predators. The giant Asian hornet cuts off other insects' heads with its sharp jaws and carries the body back to its nest to feed its larvae. Its victims include praying mantises, wasps and bees. However, Japanese honeybees have evolved a clever defence. They form a tight ball around the hornet until it dies of overheating.

This giant Asian hornet is attacking a wasp. Its 6-mm-long sting injects venom powerful enough to kill a human.

On the move

Insects get about by walking, flying, jumping, burrowing and, occasionally, swimming. The fastest runner of the insect world is the tiger beetle, a fierce predator that can run at 9 kph. Relative to its length, this is more than 20 times faster than an Olympic sprinter.

Tiger beetles use their speed, good eyesight and fast reaction times to capture prey.

Taking to the air

Most insects have four wings. When they fly, their wings move up and down, but also forwards and backwards, which allows them to perform acrobatic manoeuvres. Dragonflies are among the fastest fliers, reaching about 50 kph. Some insects shed their wings when they no longer need them. Winged ants take to the air to mate, then the males die and the females find a nesting spot and bite off their own wings.

Most four-winged insects raise and lower both pairs of wings together, but dragonflies move their two sets of wings independently. This makes them the aerial stunt artists of the insect world.

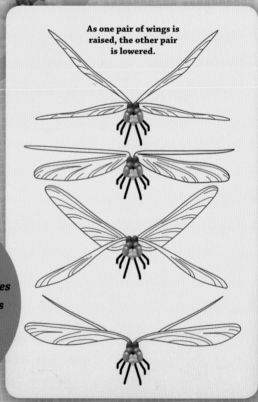

As one pair of wings is raised, the other pair is lowered.

Champion jumpers

Some insects have evolved the ability to leap impressive distances. Fleas use their jumping ability to spring aboard new host animals. Locusts can leap about two metres into the air and a grasshopper's leg muscles have ten times more power than a human's. The prize-winning jumper, however, is the little froghopper, which accelerates from the ground with a force that is 400 times greater than gravity.

Froghoppers are also known as spittlebugs. These tiny, sap-sucking insects can jump to heights of 70 cm.

Going underground

Many insects live underground, including some species of ants, bees, wasps and beetles. The mole cricket's shovel-like front legs and armoured head make it the ultimate tunnelling machine. It feeds on plant roots, larvae and worms and is rarely seen on the surface. Mole crickets can fly but they cannot jump like their close relatives.

Mole crickets spend most of their lives underground.

Adapting to extremes

There are so many different varieties of insects that they have evolved to live almost everywhere on Earth. Being small creatures, they can survive on little food and find shelter in the tiniest of spaces.

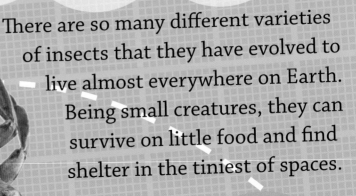

Giant water bugs have evolved to live in water. They have flattened back legs that act like oars and a snorkel-like breathing tube at the rear end of their abdomen.

Desert dwellers

Many insects have adapted to life in the desert, where most get all the water they need from their food. Some desert insects lay eggs underground, which only hatch when it rains. The young insects feed on the plants that grow during the short wet season, then lay their own eggs underground.

The desert cricket can dig a hole in the sand and disappear within seconds. It drinks the moisture that collects on plants early in the morning.

Surviving the cold

Insects are cold-blooded, which means they cannot warm themselves up in cold weather, however their bodies can withstand a wide range of temperatures. Many insects shelter underground or inside plants to escape the cold. Some Arctic beetles, bugs and lacewings have antifreeze in their blood that stops it freezing solid.

Arctic butterflies fly close to the ground, out of the icy wind. Their caterpillars hibernate during the long winter and emerge the following summer.

Life in the dark

Cave insects include cockroaches, beetles and crickets. They have adapted to the darkness and their eyes have reduced in size or totally disappeared. To make up for this, their antennae are often longer. Many cave beetles have smaller wings or have lost their wings completely because they live in small spaces with no room to fly. Cave insects are often pale in colour because they are not exposed to the Sun.

Cockroaches that live in caves feed on bat droppings, dead animals and other insects.

Living in groups

Some species of bees and wasps, along with ants and termites, live together in a colony. Each member has a part to play in maintaining and protecting the nest, finding food and raising the next generation.

Wasps build nests from chewed-up wood. The adults hunt for insects and take them back to the nest for the young to eat.

A caring community

Honeybees live in large colonies with a single queen. The female worker bees cooperate with one another to build and protect the hive. They feed and care for the young and keep them cool by beating their wings. Male bees, called drones, only have one job, which is to mate with the queen. After that, they die.

Female worker bees are responsible for finding food. If they discover a good source they fly back to the nest and perform a 'waggle dance' to tell others where it is.

Insect architects

Termites build some of the most impressive nests in the insect world. Their colonies often come under attack, particularly by ants, so they have an army of soldier termites with enlarged jaws to defend the nest. The termite king stays with his queen throughout her life and helps her to feed their young.

These massive termite mounds are in Kakadu National Park, Northern Territory, Australia.

Innumerable ants

Ants evolved from wasp-like insects around 120 million years ago. There are now an estimated 20,000 species. They live in colonies, which can have millions of members, headed by a queen or queens. The ants we see above ground are usually workers – wingless females that search for food, care for the young and defend the nest. Ants communicate with one another using chemicals called pheromones.

Leaf-cutter ants work together to carry pieces of leaf back to their nest. The ants use these to grow a fungus, which they eat.

Traps and trickery

Insects have developed a number of tricks to help them to catch prey and to avoid being eaten themselves. The flower mantis hides among plants until prey comes within reach. At the same time, the mantis is perfectly camouflaged so predators do not spot it.

head

leg

This orchid mantis is almost impossible to spot as it hides on a flower spike.

Insects in disguise

Harmless insects sometimes mimic (copy) those that are poisonous or can sting as a way of defending themselves against predators. The viceroy butterfly's orange and black wings look very like those of the poisonous monarch butterfly, for example. Many insects mimic the colours of bees or wasps so that predators think twice before attacking them.

This hoverfly could easily be mistaken for a bee, but it has no sting.

Setting a trap

The adult ant lion (above) is a flying insect similar to a dragonfly, but its larva is a fierce-looking creature with jaws like a bull's horns. The young ant lion is not fast enough to catch moving prey, so it digs a funnel-shaped pit. It buries itself at the bottom of the pit with its powerful jaws exposed, ready to snap up any insect that falls in.

An ant lion larva's jaws inject venom that dissolves the insides of its prey.

Cuckoo in the nest

The caterpillar of the Alcon blue butterfly has an outer coating of chemicals that trick ants into believing that it is one of their own larvae. When ants find the caterpillar they carry it to their nest and feed it. In the meantime, the caterpillar eats the ant larvae. When the caterpillar is fully grown, it pupates. Once the adult butterfly emerges from its pupa it must escape quickly, as without its chemical coating the ants will attack it.

The Alcon blue lays its eggs on gentian plants. When the caterpillars grow to a certain size, they drop to the ground and wait for ants to find them.

Insects are important

Insects may not be as cuddly as pandas or other **endangered** mammals, but without them we would find it difficult to survive. Insects pollinate crops, prey on other insect pests and eat rubbish, such as rotting plant material and dung.

Ladybirds are a farmer's friend. They and their larvae (shown here) have a huge appetite for insects called aphids, which damage plants.

Insects at risk

Some insects are like waste disposal units and eat anything from soap to hair. Others have very specialised diets and only eat a single type of plant. The jewel-like tansy beetle is at risk of **extinction** because tansy plants are being overgrown by Himalayan balsam, which has become a problem weed along riverbanks throughout Britain.

Tansy beetles cannot fly, so they have to search for tansy plants on foot.

Evolution in action

During the late 19th and early 20th centuries, city tree trunks became darkened by soot. In response, peppered moths developed darker-coloured wings so they could settle on the trunks without being spotted by birds. Now our cities are cleaner, the moths' wings are becoming lighter again.

The peppered moth's wings change colour in line with pollution. In more polluted areas the dark-winged moth (bottom right) is more common.

Food of the future?

Many animals – including humans in some parts of the world – eat insects. As our population grows, experts think that adding insects to the menu might be the solution to feeding all the extra people. Insects are full of goodness, breed quickly and take up little space, so grasshoppers could one day be replacing cows at a farm near you!

Insects are a popular food in Asia and Africa.

Extraordinary insects

Insects are amazingly successful creatures. Here are just a few of the many incredible facts about these magnificent mini-beasts.

Sensitive feet

Houseflies taste with their feet, which are ten million times more sensitive than our tongues.

Champion weightlifters

Ants can carry more than 50 times their own weight.

Muscular larva

A caterpillar has up to 4,000 muscles. There are almost 250 in its head and about 70 control each body segment. By comparison, a human has just 629.

Killer bugs

By spreading diseases such as malaria, mosquitoes have killed more people than all the wars in history.

Hard-working bees

A bee has to visit 4,000 flowers to make just one tablespoon of honey.

Towering nest

The tallest termite's nest was more than 12 metres high.

Massive swarm

A swarm of locusts can contain up to 40 billion insects.

Collective intelligence

A colony of 40,000 ants has the same brain power as a human.

Heavyweight cricket

The heaviest insect is the giant weta (below), which at 71 g weighs three times more than a mouse. The cricket-like creature likes to eat carrots and is found only on Little Barrier Island, New Zealand.

Glossary

Adapt To adjust to new conditions

Antennae A pair of long feelers on an insect's head that can sense touch, movement, heat and vibrations, and are used to smell and taste

Camouflage Natural colouring that allows an animal to blend in with its surroundings

Chrysalis The pupa of a butterfly or moth

Cold-blooded An animal whose body temperature changes according to the surrounding air or water temperature

Colonise To become established in an area

Cretaceous period 145–66 million years ago

Endangered At risk of dying out completely

Evolve To develop gradually over generations

Exoskeleton An outer shell that supports and protects an insect's body

Extinction When all living members of a species have died out

Fertilisation The process that happens when pollen and the female part of a plant join together to make a seed

Fossil The preserved remains or impression of animals and plants that died long ago

Generation Animals born and living at about the same time

Gills The organs used by underwater creatures to absorb oxygen from the water

Hibernate Go into a deep sleep to survive the cold weather when food is scarce

Host An animal or plant that a parasite lives in or on

Invertebrate An animal without a backbone

Jurassic period 201–145 million years ago

Larva A young insect, such as a caterpillar

Mate One of a pair of animals that produce young together, or to produce young

Migrate Move from one area to another according to the seasons, usually to find food

Nocturnal Active during the night

Nymph A young insect that does not undergo complete metamorphosis

Parasite An animal that lives in or on another creature and feeds on that creature

Pollinate To carry pollen to a flower so it can be fertilised and produce seeds

Predator An animal that hunts other creatures for food

Pupa An insect enclosed in a hard case while it changes from a larva to an adult

Resin A sticky substance produced by some trees and plants

Social insects Insects that live in groups and cooperate to care for the young

Species A group of animals that can breed with one another and produce healthy babies, which are able to breed when they grow up

Triassic period 248–201 million years ago

Vertebrate An animal with a backbone

Index

Find out more

Here are some useful websites to help you learn more about insects and evolution.

 http://animals.nationalgeographic.co.uk/animals/bugs

 www.nhm.ac.uk/nature-online/life/insects-spiders

 www.bbc.co.uk/nature/life/Insect   www.buglife.org.uk